THE MAGIC OF THE RED DRESS

**Rhymes about Women
Who Helped Tame the West**

Judie Cole and Louise Halotek

To Shannon
Judie

With Illustrations by
Wendy Port
and
Cover Photography by
John Halotek III

2021 by Judie Cole and Louise Halotek
All rights reserved. No part of this book may be reproduced, stored in a retrieval system or transmitted in any form without the prior written permission of the publishers, except by a reviewer who may quote brief passages in a review to be printed in a newspaper, magazine or journal.

First printing.

All characters in this book are fictitious, and any resemblance to real persons, living or dead, is coincidental.

ISBN: 978-1-66780-862-8

We wish to express our appreciation to a couple of entities who influenced and supported our efforts to realize our dream of writing Poetry about the Old West.

The Durango Cowboy Poetry Gathering, which we attended on many occasions, introduced us to storytelling of western life in poetry and music form. Hearing the stories of the Old West in lyric fashion was intriguing to us. We were compelled to give it a try. The following poems are the result of that effort. We performed some of our poems several times at the Gathering at the historic Strater Hotel in Durango. We, also, attended the Wickenberg Poetry Gathering and were thrilled by other fine poets.

We want to acknowledge the support of our husbands who travelled with us to The Gathering. They listened over and over to new ideas, new lines and new poems. They even tried to help us write…..help which we rejected as this was, after all, our project! They always encouraged us to write more and we did. A western party was held on one occasion so we could introduce our poetry to our friends. Thanks to them for listening so enthusiastically.

Our greatest thanks goes to the women of the Old West who inspired us as no other subject could. Consequently, many of our poems are about them and the roles they played as wives, daughters, mothers, and ladies of saloon life. Their lives were truly challenging. Hopefully our poetry will give some understanding of the vital place they have in our history of the taming of the west,

Judie and Louise

For our husbands who enthusiastically supported us by accompanying us to various events, attending our presentations, and most of all, listening to new lines, new ideas and new poems. They were particularly supportive of our interest in and passion to write about the women of the old west. For all of this and more we are very grateful.

TABLE
OF
CONTENTS

Part One

Part Two

Part Three

THE MAGIC of the RED DRESS

Rhymes about Women Who Helped Tame the West

Part One

MISS
TESS

She was born in a cabin
   under a Comanche moon
Within earshot of Indians dancing and drumming
The brightness of the sky signaled trouble
A raid at this time could cause double
The loss of cattle, horses or winter storage

When Ma Sarah and Pa Tom saw her
   they started humming
It soon would be time for a name to be coming
She emerged as Tess
   all hoping, for her, the very best

At an early age she began singing and strumming
She learned her chores during the day
There wasn't much time for little Tess to play

The animals on the ranch were her playmates
She didn't have time for friends or dates
The sun, moon and stars were her light
She continued to sing and dance into the night

She learned riding and roping,
as well as loping
She combed the plains and hills
for strays
Bringing them home to rest
in the bays

Roaming the range far and wide
With her trusty old dog
by her side
She came upon ranchers and
wranglers with nothing
to hide
The stories they told her were
easy to bide
Full of history, tradition and tales
of their drives

Sounds of cattle lowing,
blackbirds singing
and cowboy lore
Gave her exciting thoughts
she'd never had before

One day she traveled into town
In the rickety buckboard with
the top down
Gazing at the shops
and the stores
She found the scene
quite amazing
The blazing colors and the
sounds of hustle
Oh, how she wanted a
red dress with a bustle

The children played with a colorful balloon
While across the street was the
   Diamond Belle Saloon
The saloon door creaked open and closed
Her curiosity got the best of her
So she poked in her nose

There were poker-face men and beautiful women
Gathered around a huge curved bar
Everyone listening to a strumming guitar
Tess knew at that moment what she needed to do
Buy a red dress and some fancy toed shoes

And soon enough she entered the saloon
And started dancing in the light of the moon
All the while singing a honky-tonk tune
Tess thought to herself, how beautiful I am…
As the creaky door opened
 in walked COWBOY SAM

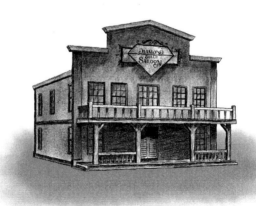

He was known as Cowboy Sam
 the quiet man
A lonely man, out at night, with only a blanket,
 his horse, his gun,
And the moon for light

It wasn't an easy life
 but he didn't care
Even if others thought life was unfair
He loved the stars and the solitude
He bathed in the river
 Always in the nude

Food was aplenty,
 dried beef, berries, rattlesnake and
 occasionally a poppy seed cake
Sometimes he found jerky or even a wild turkey

One day Sam wandered into town…
    feeling low…
    feeling down…
When he spied Miss Tess in her bright red dress
He nodded "Howdy", then headed for the bar
Where he grabbed a pickled egg
    straight from the jar

He knew he was staying when the music started playing
    rinky tink piano, a shot and a beer…
    hello friend, Cowboy Sam is here
Maybe this is the place I ought to be
He thought with a smile and a slight sneer
Miss Tess, the music and the booze
Were a powerful strong ruse

When Miss Tess
started to sing
Sam began to
dance along
They danced and
they twirled and
finally spent
the night
Lordy it was a
beautiful sight

No longer was Sam a quiet man
He kicked up his heels squealing
  'yippee-yi-ki-yay'
Had he seen a new light,
    was he preparing to take flight
From his old ways, the trail, the
    mountains, the cows and
    his old bay

Sam opened his eyes once again to
    the sun rising across the terrain
Remembering his old friends out
    on the plain

Miss Tess in her lovely red dress
    and her life filled with fun
Couldn't compare with the run
    of the herd
The coolness of the mountain
    breeze or warmth
    of a campfire

Looking forward to the next year
He gathered his gear and headed
    out of town
And thus began…
    the one night stand

Cowboy Sam awoke
with a start
Something new had
happened to his heart
But…
As the sun rose and he saw
the snow had begun to fall
He once again could feel
the "call"
Causing him to prepare
to head for his bay and
his steer
He gathered his gear and kissed
Miss Tess on the ear
Promising he would try to stay near

It was in the spring when the grass was green
And the dandelions grew by the side of a stream
They met again, perhaps by chance
And soon began to sing and dance

Sam with a smile three yards wide asked
   Miss Tess to be his bride
Under the white gown with Sam by her side
Grew two little babies only inches wide

On a windy snowy night
When all the leaves of fall had taken flight
The embers in the fire were just a smolder
When Tess tapped Sam on the shoulder
Sam "it's time" she said and Sam rose quickly
   out of bed
The time had come…

Early on a Sunday morn
   when church bells rang
A child was born…
   moments later another one
First a daughter…
   then a son
Bess and Jess were their names
Life from this day forward would never
   be the same

Sam pondered the two little miracles
Not horses, cows or even fame
Nothing could compare with this claim
There was a mysterious hand at play
    in what many thought of as....
One night in the hay

JAKE

Sitting alone in the loft strumming a song
Hoping no one else would soon come along
Especially not his Grandpa Sam or Dad
Because his inner thoughts were making him sad

His future was destined to be cattle and crops
Just like his Grandpa Sam and his Pops
But his thoughts strayed to more exciting things
Such as riding and roping in a red shirt with bling

Barrels, wild bulls....
    horse and ropes
And riding as fast as a scary ghost
Those are the tools he thought about most

Time to go back to work
Feeding the cattle and
    "slopping" the pork
Hoeing the crops and
    cutting the wood
All this was
    expected of a son
    who was good

When it was time to let his family know
That his job was not at the home, but at the Rodeo
So many lights and lots of fun were all part of the show
Just thinking about it set him aglow

Late tonight he planned to leave the farm
Hoping not to cause any harm
He'd ride and rope those huge fierce bulls
Hoping he would not become a fool

Now with a plan and a little luck
He would act with glory and not end in the muck
After a time all would know
How great a talent had been bestowed

Ma, Pa and Grandpa Sam would see
How life on the farm could not be
His thoughts were interrupted by a voice
Now he had to make an important choice

He descended his perch in the loft of hay
To tell his family of his thoughts of today
Down below were Grandpappy and Pops
They shouted hello as his feet dropped

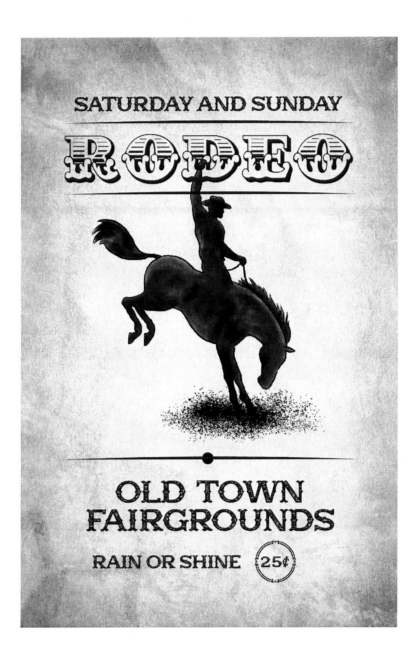

SATURDAY AND SUNDAY

RODEO

OLD TOWN
FAIRGROUNDS

RAIN OR SHINE 25¢

They greeted Jake with friendly throngs
Saying they heard his mournful song
Soon he thought he heard them say
Today is a very very special day

At the edge of town at the big fairgrounds
Lots of fun and noise were expected to abound
With many riders and animals renown
The rodeo had at last arrived in town

They wondered if Jake would like to go and give it a try
'Cause they knew he was a very talented guy
He rode and roped like a winner they said
Not at all like a beginner who stays in bed

His happiness overwhelmed him
What he heard confirmed this was not a whim
And his Ma was holding a beautiful red shirt
   decorated with bling

Late that night his Pa came to him
And said he knew the chances were slim
That life on the ranch was for him

The Magic of the Red Dress

OF THE

Red Dress

Rhymes about Women
Who Helped Tame the West

PART TWO

Many stories are told about the men of old
Who may have gone west to find gold
Work by day and play by night
Didn't fill them with delight

The Last Chance Saloon opened its doors
Offering the usual stores
Whiskey and gin to brighten the evening
Although music and gambling filled the hall
The Cowboys and miners were not having a ball
Alas…The barkeep put out a call
For ladies with curls and young maiden girls

Working the farm and fearing some harm
The young widow, Rose, knew she needed to go
Having just left her shabby home
She stepped from the wagon…
    poor and alone
Dressed in all brown from
    toe to crown
She resembled a woman
    of great renown
Her dress and her pose caused
her to become Cinnamon Rose

Miss Kitty arrived from the city with dog
    Princess by her side
She headed west in a hurry…
    there was nowhere to hide
A new life to start
She arrived in town with a broken heart
She saw the sign for the Last Chance Saloon
    and started to hum a merry tune

Up on the hill
Giving all a thrill
Was the carriage of none other than Diamond Lil
She descended to town
Wearing a lovely red gown
She planned to offer song and dance
To the boys at the Last Chance

They all arrived together to the barkeep's surprise
There was no way he could deny
Hiring them all he would fill the hall

On opening night the bill highlighted
   Cinnamon Rose, Miss Kitty and Diamond Lil

Out on the streets the line began to form
All anticipating the sound of the horn
The door opened to reveal
Three beautiful ladies in high heels

Shouts of joy could be heard far and wide
As soon as the ladies were by their sides

The music began and the liquor flowed
When up on the stage Diamond Lil strode

As Lil sang a soulful ballad
Cinnamon Rose danced with Simon Allard
Miss Kitty sitting at the bar eyed the Sheriff from afar
He sauntered toward her with a grin
And immediately ordered a shot of gin

Fortified with booze
He thought Kitty a potential muse
He approached her with hat in hand
Promising to act on her command
Kitty ascended the stairs with a swish of her red skirt
Flashing all patrons a little flirt

At the end of the evening all the fervor was gone
The boys headed home, to work another day
The ladies, though tired, decided to stay
There WAS a place for them in the west
All they wanted to do was give their best

MISS KITTY

Kitty ascended the stairs with a swish of her red skirt
Flashing all the patrons a flirt
Something she had never done before
While working in that awful store

Don't think of the store she reminded herself
Life in the past must be put on a shelf
Escape from swarthy Jim, she thought her
  chances very slim
The money her father owed she could not pay
Kitty had refused a lay in the hay

The day she and her dog had to run away
Her heart beat fast and her legs felt like clay
Chasing and chasing, hoping to escape this day
Causing her to become pale and in dismay
Careful hiding, maneuvering and jumping onto the rail
Had caused old Jim in his pursuit to fail

After a day and a night, the train
landed her in a new town
She descended the car dreaming of
finding a beautiful
red gown
Wanting as always a life filled
with renown
But woe and alas she had no money, only her
usual genteel class

Rising above her flew a beautiful red balloon
Launched from the town's only saloon
An idea formed at that time in
her mind
Maybe no longer necessary to work in a
store and endure the grind
She decided never again to look behind

The doors were swinging in the wind
Luring her to enter in
Greeted by gaiety and light, the darkness she expected was
   not her plight
All hailed her howdy and pulled her in,
Including Cinnamon Rose, Lil and even little Gwin

She had found her destiny
Away from her troubles and bad men
With friends to guide her
And keep her safely
   at a ten

DIAMOND LIL

She was born Lillian West on a hot summer day
Remembering as a child she had few toys to play
Her mother always dressed in diamonds and furs
Seemed to have very little time for her

Alone at home one wintery day
She took out the diamonds and started to play
They sparkled and shimmered on her neck and ears
Seeing such beauty, she was drawn to tears

Over and over she saw in the glass
A little girl transformed into a beautiful lass
And in her eyes a dream began to form
She saw a beauty emerging above the norm
Lil longed for the day when all
would be hers
And she would own
the diamonds and furs

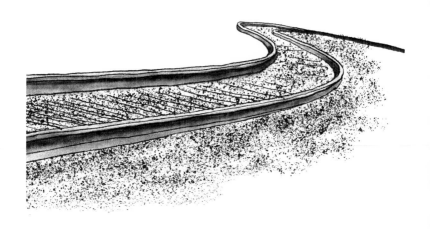

All too soon to Lil's dismay
Her mother's life slipped away
A horse and buggy went astray
As she was riding one fine day

Grief and memories flooded her nights
Bringing her to make plans to take flight
Clackety clack, clackety clack the sounds
    of the train on the track
The noise caused ideas to grow in her mind

Dressed in her best she boarded the train heading west
Determined to look her very best
She held her diamonds and furs close to her chest

The train slowed in a small town
Before her final destination was found
Although west bound… she was tired and down
Surprisingly the sign above read
  "Looking for Ladies of Renown"

Tiredly she climbed the high stairs
Fixed on dinner, a bath and combing her hair
Her elegance and beauty had drawn the attention
of the brothel Madam
When she entered the huge red door which made
  a loud slam
She was greeted by Madam, who wanted to talk
And insisted on taking a very short walk

The stories Madam Olivia told, were very much
  like pure liquid gold
She told tales of ranchers, gamblers and miners
With purses filled with coins and beautiful gems
Just like the ones she had sewn into her hems

Madam Olivia continued to explain
About the importance of feminine gifts on the plains
Fun, frivolity and tender love needed to be offered
To these men, who had much money in their coffers

Happiness and ideas began to arise
Maybe this trip would not be her demise
She had much to learn while honing her skill
All the time increasing the amount in her till

Time passed quickly while she learned her trade
Finally, she decided to head further west and see
    this town fade
With more coins in her purse and more gems in her hems
She boarded the train and said goodbye to her friends

Heading further west once again
Her time here really was a win
She felt now that she could fulfill her goal
Hot in her mind as a heater full of coal

Her dream included a lovely "house"
Filled to the brim with not one mouse
But, with a passel of beautifully dressed ladies
Who would entertain the town's rich mateys

She saw herself in her gems and jewels
Encouraging the patrons to have fun not duels
She asked herself if this would work
Of course it would she thought with a smirk

Destination west came very soon
Only a day and a half about noon
Thinking of exploring and looking around
She saw many possibilities abound

Here spirits were high and so confident
She was sure this is what her dreams had meant
The town was filled with smells of cattle, horses
    and mountain breezes
Walking around, her throbbing heart practically seizes

Right in front of her very nose
Was a beautiful house with a Victorian pose
The sign in front said "For Sale"
Immediately she stopped and gave a huge wail
"I must see this perfect place without fail"
She filled her house with drinkers, gamblers
    and women in fancy clothes
Fun and frivolity in the brothel finally arose

Later in her room her thoughts turned to her mother
Her lively spirit and presence always seemed to hover
Encouraging her this night to take the stage,
    dressed in a beautiful red dress
Singing and dancing made her the new rage

With dreams fulfilled and a very full till
She walked around town to the top of the hill
And giving thanks to one and all
At last she was the Belle of the Ball

Simon Allard

This is a sonnet or maybe a ballad
Of an undercover Pinkerton agent called Simon Allard
He wears a badge and carries two great big guns
He fights for justice and causes bad guys to run

His hat is black and he has a scar on his cheek
Considered handsome causing women to take a long peek
His clothes are dusty and pretty worn
His saddle, however, has a silver trimmed horn

Simon's best friend is his beautiful brown mare
When he's on the hunt, those men on wanted posters
    don't have a prayer
He's tough but always fights fair
Even when he's outnumbered and has to approach a
    thieves' lair

He works day and night
    carrying out the law
Never having time to
    say a "hurrah"
As time passes this makes
    him feel sad
Seeing others engaged in
    life's pursuits makes
    him glad

Sitting by his campfire one spring evening at sundown
Contemplating his next assignment with a frown
He began to dream of life and land
Not possible for me he concluded, before these thoughts
    were banned

Justice and a dangerous life on the hunt
That's my world he countered with a grunt
The sheriffs and judges were counting on him
To bring to justice very evil men

Day after day he rode the hills and plains
Killing or capturing and putting men in chains
But night after night his thoughts returned to life
Causing him some bit of worry and strife

As Simon on his horse approached the new town
He paused to take a quick look around
Peace and tranquility seemed to abound
Not even a stray cat or skinny hound

People walking here and there
Sounds of music heard everywhere
Why not treat myself to a little drink
It's been too long since he heard two glasses clink

Into the saloon he slowly went
With his head a little bit bent
Unsure of what he might find
But what he saw nearly blew his mind

A big beautiful polished wood bar
People laughing, gambling and singing were par
Lovely ladies talking here and there
Some even hugging as though they were a pair

Descending the curved stairway was someone so fair
She was a woman of beauty with long chestnut hair
Her loveliness stopped him in his tracks
Simon felt as though he had fallen into a crack
Bar keep, bar keep!! Who is that woman of great repose
Well sir...that is Cinnamon Rose

From the crest of the hill he saw the homestead below
Moving the cattle had been very slow
A long time away
Made this a very special day

Wild Will, as he was known, headed down the hill
When the noise behind him began to build
The cattle were running much too fast
This speed and recklessness could not last

Rose watched from the window with fear in her eyes
She heard a terrible thunder and saw the dust arise
Will, Will…get them under control!
It was a horrible scene for her to behold

When the stampede was over
Cowboy Will lay amongst the clover
After the dust had cleared there could be no disguise
Rose saw her husband
Dead…she surmised

Sadness overtook her everyday life
She was no longer a beloved wife
She sewed a dress of beautiful brown
To wear to bury her man of renown

Wearing the dress of rich golden brown
And leading a procession from the town
They buried dear Will…a man without foes
And began referring to his wife as Cinnamon Rose

So much time passed and increased her woes
Shabby property and financial blows
She needed a new life
She was no longer protected as a wife

Afraid her pain would draw terrible predators
Rose felt she needed to run from her creditors
She packed her things and headed for a new home
Confused and sad she began to roam

A wagon approached going further west
She hurried and made herself look her very best
In hopes that asking to join, could accomplish her quest
The answer was, yes, and she felt blessed

The trail was dusty
And the wagon rusty
Day after day she rode, being jostled from side to side
Often sleeping under only an animal hide

Doubts began to cloud her mind
Was this the route to leave her woes behind

Off in the distance was a town of some size
Her spirits soared to this wonderful surprise
Amongst the dust of the movement in town
She noticed the sign which caused her to dance
    like a clown

The Last Chance Saloon with its fancy red door
Had a sign in front causing her to worry no more
They were looking for ladies with beauty,
    grace and talent galore
She knew she'd fit in with the glamorous décor

Within hours, she made her play
Within minutes she was hired by Bartender Clay
She danced and sang and brought happiness over all
She took her place as another of the Belles of the Ball

THE MAGIC
OF THE
RED DRESS

Rhymes about Women
Who Helped Tame the West

PART
THREE

THE MAKING OF AN OUTLAW

WANTED
DEAD OR ALIVE

$1,000 REWARD

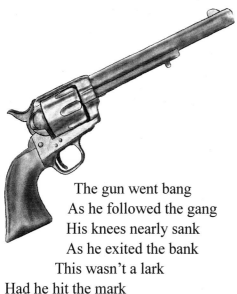

The gun went bang
As he followed the gang
His knees nearly sank
As he exited the bank
This wasn't a lark
Had he hit the mark
His eyes were wide, like a huge shark

Oh by golly, what have I done

He headed for home and hid in the barn
Wishing this some sort of yarn
He knew he would be safe at the farm

What have I seen and what have I done

He heard them before he could see them
He was awakened by the rumble of the horses
Lots of scraggly unkempt men
Were these the sounds of evil forces

He burrowed deeply in the pen
It wasn't a joke, he was smelling smoke

What have I done

The fire grew higher and the flames burned hot
He raced from the barn to find a new spot
Safely in the woods, he hid from the hoods

Fear engulfed his body and mind
Knowing he was leaving his beloved home behind

Had a new life begun

He was now on the run
So without kit nor kin and
His mind full of his sin
He knew not how he could win

Oh my goodness, he was not yet a man
He did not want to spend life in a pen
Especially when he was only ten!

THE SALOON

The door creaks when it opens, the secrets lure them inside
The noise is deafening, gaiety and merriment thrive
Hats and guns are laid aside to be traded for easier lives
Kings and Queens reign supreme not in a castle or a keep
But just until aces are thrown on the heap
Voices are raised in rousing song, a great release for the
growing throng
Ladies and gents swing and sway, some finding special
places to play
Many come in and they go out, often with a raucous shout
Whiskey and gin in here are not a sin, they are considered
the ultimate win
Some leave walking and some leave drunk, followed by their
belongings and sometimes a trunk
The upstairs is quiet with passion and play, for the ladies it's
just another working day

Cattle and horses are traded and discussed, money changes
hands after quite a fuss
Some happy with the deal and some not so much
This place is the heartbeat of our little town, bringing
friends, foes and even some who are renowned
Stories, lies and tales of woe fill the air, while the
hurdy-gurdy plays with a flare
Beautiful dancers bump and grind, as the barkeep holds the
men in line
Out in the street, the passersby hum a tune
Saturday night, at the Happy Valley Saloon

You're feckless and reckless his friend said to him,
   as he pulled in his chips
His fingers easily manipulating the coins, his smile
   curved his crooked lips
His response was short, almost a snort

No one knows who I am, or that I'm on the lam
They will take one look at me wearing this coat
Smelling a bit like an old goat

They expect to win against me as the cards are dealt
Betting their money and sometimes their pelts
The cards keep coming to their surprise
 I show them mine to their demise

Just random luck, nothing more they proclaim
A man like you cannot be to blame
We'll put to rest this streak of yours
Then you can leave and do your chores

Chores! What little you men know
My winnings are going to continue to grow
No more chores for me

Only open doors and hefty roars as I take my place
No one can keep pace
After today my reputation will preceed me far and wide
Causing players to run and hide,
Unable to risk the losing tide

Game after game was won and lost, everyone knowing
      who was boss
As my stack grew higher, there were those who wondered
      if I was a liar
They began to question my talk of cattle drives, horses
      and hay stores

Then suddenly there erupted a series of roars
All I could hear was the sound of a gun, and soon
      the darkening of the sun
Someone has shot me, I realize with surprise
They wish only of my demise, is this the end of my luck

I'm lying here alone in the filthy muck, attended only
   by my friend Buck
Thoughts continue to swim in my head,
   my dreams becoming fuzzy
I realize with dread....
   I think I'm dead

Would I Complain

I sat and wondered what it was like
To travel west in a stagecoach at night
Over the mountains and the plains

    Would I complain

What was it like to see the stars
The distant mountains from afar
The trails of mud, mountains with snow
I was young, what did I know

    Would I Complain

You would learn a lot in those days
Cooking the grub, riding in the coach and
  chasing the strays
No time to play

    No Time to Complain

What would it be like bumping along, while
    singing a silly song

Watching shadows as they grew long
Feeling the breeze from side curtains open wide
Listening to Buck, our wise guide
As he shared stories, making me want to hide
So shaking with fear it became clear, I would
　have to be brave
And learn how to behave

　　Would I Complain

When we arrived at our designated spot
Our horses tired and hungry and so much to do
Overwhelmed by great beauty and a sense of duty
Our hearts became alive, with hopes to survive

I guess there would be no need to Complain!!!

The Dreamer

I lay tonight filled with fright
Looking left and looking right
Wondering from where on the prairie vast
Came that lovely vision whizzing past

An enchanting sound encircled me
Continuing to go round and round
Seeing something, like a beautiful crown
Accompanied by a vision in a red flowing gown

Slowly the vision began to scatter
With a wave to the north
And a curve to the south

It tumbled and swirled and moved in time
Somewhere inside me, a feeling occurred
Leaving my heartbeat high, and feeling a glow
I fell off to sleep without a word

Sunrise came and I was solely surrounded by my men
    and a herd of cows
Each lifted its head in greeting and lowered it in a bow
No enchanting sounds or flowing gowns were around
How did it all happen, when nothing was to be found

Exhausting my body and mind by hard work
Riding the range and tending the cows wherever they lurk
Made me think I was a contented man
Employing a sound life plan

Night again and my heart beats fast
The cows abed and the men down at last
Drifting off to slumber and hopefully good dreams
I feel a gentle breeze going past
She brushed her lips across my chin
Oh, what a romantic mood I'm in

The movement and motion filled him with pride
What's this all about?
Am I thinking of taking a bride?

A COWBOY'S CHRISTMAS

The sky is inky dark
No sounds except a coyote's bark
The moon and stars are out of sight
I can't tell if I'm riding left or right

On this mystical eve of my Savior's birth
I find myself without much mirth
All the time feeling I am alone on this earth
Longing to be home by our cozy stone hearth

Sadness engulfs my body and mind
For all the joys I've left behind
Christmas lights and laughter filling the air
Smells of baking and foods made with holiday care

Riding up and riding down, trying not to cry or frown
While calculating the time to the rancher's town
With serious thoughts of returning home
I respond with a loud moan
To the sound of a mountain lion's groan

The cattle become nervous and begin to veer
To protect themselves from what they hear
The dogs are running this way and that, keeping
  order in spite of the cat

All at once the sky begins to clear
The brightness reveals the destination is near
A special star seems to be lighting the way
Just as it did on that famous day
When a precious new life was laid on the hay
Quite a way, I guess, to begin the celebration
  of Christmas Day